Playgrounds

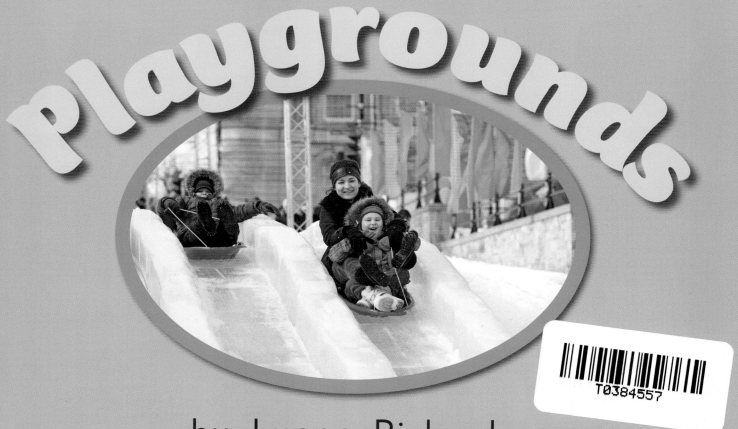

by Lynne Rickards

CAMBRIDGE
UNIVERSITY PRESS

UCL
Institute of Education

Playgrounds are safe places for children to play.

Some playgrounds are made of wood.
They look like a fort or a tree house.

This playground is made to look like a ship.

This playground looks like a castle.

Children can go inside.

The sun can get very hot.
A playground needs shade.

Children can cool down in the water.

This slide looks like a red snake.
Children can slide down.

Some playgrounds are made of ice.

Children can slide very fast.

Children can play inside when it rains.

It's fun to play in the balls.

What can you do in these playgrounds?

Playgrounds Lynne Rickards

Teaching notes written by Sue Bodman and Glen Franklin

Using this book

Developing reading comprehension

This non-chronological report explores some important features of playgrounds; how they look, where they are and what children can do. The reader is required to have control of print location and one-to-one correspondence as the text appears at both the top and bottom of the page, with some sentences going on to two lines of text.

Grammar and sentence structure

- Some repetition of phrase patterns commonly used in reporting genres ('*Some playgrounds are*'; '*This playground is*').

- Punctuation and line placement support the development of phrased reading.

- Sentence structures typical of non-fiction reports ('*Children can*') with some use of familiar oral language ('*It's fun*').

Word meaning and spelling

- Opportunity to rehearse a wide range of known high frequency words ('*can*', '*look*', '*like*', '*made*')

- Practice and consolidation of reading regular decodable words

- Opportunity to use print detail to read for the precise meaning ('*in*', *inside*')

Curriculum links

Language Development – Speaking and Listening activities could develop the use of simile. In the book, '*This slide looks like a red snake*'. Photographs or pictures on iPads could be used for discussion, for example, 'This path looks like (a winding snake, a wiggly worm).', 'The moon looks like... (a shining light, a yellow mirror, a piece of cheese)'.

Mathematics – The playgrounds have slides, tunnels and turrets. The pictures could be used to reinforce the naming vocabulary of three dimensional solid shapes – cylinder, cuboid, sphere, cube, triangular prism.

Learning Outcomes

Children can:

- read aloud using the context, sentence structure and sight vocabulary to read with expression and for meaning

- attempt new words in more challenging texts using phonic knowledge

- comment on the information in the text, making links to their own experience.

A guided reading lesson

Book Introduction

Give each child a book and read the title to them. Activate the children's prior knowledge. Say: *Have you ever been to a playground? What was it like? Did it have any colourful or unusual things to play on?* Discuss the children's experiences making sure that the vocabulary used in the book is utilised (*slide, playground, play, safe place*).

Orientation

Give a brief overview of the book, using the verb in the continuous present tense form as it is used in the text. *There are lots of different playgrounds in this book. Let's see if they look like playgrounds you have been to.*

Preparation

Page 2: Tell the children: *It is important that children are safe when they are playing. Find the words in the text that say 'safe places'.* Say the words slowly several times and ask *What letters would you expect to see?* Praise the children for locating the words correctly and for slowly articulating to check.

Page 3: *It is also important that the children have fun. What do you think this playground looks like? Yes, that's right, it looks like a tree house or a fort. What sort of games could you play here?*

Carry on through pages 4 and 5 drawing out a description of the playground using the language structure '*It looks like a ....*'